All Scripture references taken from the KJV of the Holy Bible, unless otherwise indicated.

Gang Ups & Mobs: *Touch Not God's Anointed*

by Dr. Marlene Miles

Freshwater Press 2024

freshwaterpress9@gmail.com

ISBN: 978-1-963164-46-6

eBook Version

Copyright 2024, Dr. Marlene Miles

All rights reserved. No part of this book may be reproduced, distributed, or transmitted by any means or in any form including photocopying, recording or other electronic or mechanical methods without prior written permission of the publisher except in the case of brief publications or critical reviews.

Table of Contents

- **Destiny Is Divine** 4
- **Lucifer Didn't** 9
- **Anointed Ones** 11
- **Repent** 23
- **He Knew Us** 30
- **Whose *Will*?** 32
- **Not Interchangeable** 34
- **Too Much Witchcraft** 37
- **But *Why*?** 42
- **Soulish Prayers** 47
- **Two Or More** 49
- **The Unfriendly Friend** 51
- **Pride & the Fake Friend** 55
- **Prayers Against Unfriendly Friends** 62
- **Goodbye Gang Ups** 68
- **A Mob & Serpents** 71
- **Why Gang Ups** 80
- **Prayers Against Gang Ups** 87
- *Dear Reader* 99
- **Other books by this author** 100

Gang Ups & Mobs
Touch Not God's Anointed

Destiny Is Divine

Every man, every woman, every person is born with a destiny. Do not think that Destiny is optional because it is not. It's something you can do if you want, something you may try if you have time, or pursue if you feel like it? As if it's a college degree program and you can select your own major. No, it's not optional and your destiny has been predetermined for you by God, that you should walk in it.

> For we are his workmanship, created in Christ Jesus unto good works, which God hath before ordained that we should walk in them. (Ephesians 2:10)

What is put in you to select is *from* God. Who God made you is why you will select what you select to be, unless you are forced to do otherwise, or totally deceived into denying your true self and calling. God put the selections and the gifts, tools, and anointing to do that thing and become what He has for you to do in you.

Each person's destiny is God's purpose for our individual lives. It is our God-ordained future. If you compare what you think is a reasonable or okay future, or what you think a person of your status or lack of status could become, it will pale in comparison to what God has planned for you and how God sees you. God sees you as the finished and completed you, not the you that you are right now. God sees you through the eyes of Destiny.

God, through His Wisdom has designed you to do what you do, both in the natural, in your secular vocations, and also spiritually. In all of that there is overlap and interface, and only God knows how to make it all work for every man.

Everyone has a ministry.

Everyone.

Destiny is what God has destined us to become in His divine will and Wisdom. Each of us is also destined to do certain things, perform certain duties in our lives; this is our ministry. God has an entire plan for the Earth and for mankind. We all have something to do – not just the fivefold ministry gifts, but everyone, every gift, and even lay people.

Touch not God's anointed.

Do we dare think that the Destiny that is prepared and planned for each of us is *not* anointed. Destiny is anointed; therefore, we don't dare to touch, ruin, steal, cancel, exchange or *manipulate* the **Destiny** of another person. Do we dare push people out of their destiny? Anyone who has been discouraged, shut down or sat down, especially in a church, knows what I'm talking about.

Anyone who has been discouraged or maligned by parents or friends instead of encouraged to do and be themselves also knows what I'm talking about. That is a hard mountain to scale again if you've ever been pushed off of it.

Some get knocked down or sat down and never get back up because of naysayers, destiny takers and destroyers. Some evil and ignorant will try to convince you that you don't even have a destiny. Those are the folks who condemn others by saying, *You'll never amount to anything.*

That is NOT true, and don't you believe it.

For I know the plans I have for you," declares the LORD, "plans to

prosper you and not to harm you,
plans to give you hope and a future.
(Jeremiah 29:11)

Destiny is a holy, divine thing, we cannot treat it as if it is not. In the natural a son will take seriously the career that his own father plans for him, especially if the son is taking over the family business. He would soberly honor his father's request as long as he could do it and it is in his heart and soul to follow after his father's vocation.

We are sons of God. Shall we not take seriously what God tells us is the vocation (ministry) which we have been created and built for?

Lucifer didn't. Lucifer rebelled and ***didn't***.

We should be nothing like Lucifer.

Lucifer Didn't

We aren't Lucifer.

Lucifer was created by God and built for a certain and specific purpose, but he chose to follow *his own will*, his own path and look where it got Lucifer. He even got a name change: Satan. If you get a name change to the negative, you are really in trouble.

Captives got name changes.

Slaves got name changes.

Fallen angels got name changes; Lucifer's name was changed to Satan.

We can't disrespect what God called us to do and created us for as if it is not a holy thing, a divine thing, a God-ordained thing, because it is.

When God changes your name, it is for good and for Godly purpose. Abram's name changed to Abraham. Jacob's name was changed to Israel. Benoni's name was changed to Benjamin (Genesis 35:18). Jabez prayed and asked God that his name be changed (1 Chronicles 4:9-10). God did not change Jabez's name, but He changed his future.

Saul, persecutor of Christians, had a name change to Paul, and Simon's name was changed to Peter. There are others, I'm sure, but if God has changed your name, then destiny is not just pursuing, it is on your heels, even nigh thee.

Anointed Ones

When a person gets saved, they are immediately **anointed**. First of all, there is an anointing to *be* saved. They are an anointed one. Therefore, once this person is saved, everything about that person, their spirit, soul, body, purpose, destiny, future, career, education, spouse, family, ministry, is anointed. God then says, ***This one is in,*** like a coach, ***I can put him or her in the game.***

But God puts you in the game in your proper spiritual image, not as a baby Christian. This is why baby Christians who are ready for this, that, or the other don't do things – they are not ready, and they are not in the game as a toddler Christian. God puts you in the game in what you are supposed to be, and will be as a finished saint of God. Now you have to work at being yourself. If all of Earth is a board game, which it is not, but if it were --, God is playing with fully built pieces, not half built parts and pieces. God is playing for the win. Even though God is not playing, He is operating His plan for mankind and the Earth for the win with completed, whole, working pieces.

See that you become whole. See that you are operational, and you work. See that you are fully built up to what God has called you to be. See that you win.

Anointing is an empowerment. Do we use it? Or do we let it go to waste? We will touch on that in this book, but mostly we will talk about those who oppose God's anointing, and God's anointed.

Anointing is not just for the 5-fold ministry people in the Church. God anoints all His people so they can reach their destiny.

At salvation, we are anointed to *become* sons of God, and we are anointed for purpose and destiny. All of this takes time, so don't think that after you get saved on Sunday you are ready to do ministry on Monday. You must be prepared, get prepared, and learn. Some need deliverance first. Anointing is for preparation first, then it is for giving out ministry, gifts of the Spirit, and good works to others.

There are many different kinds and levels of anointing. Yes, it takes anointing and power to be saved. Recall that we must be forgiven our sins when we also ask Jesus to come into our hearts. Jesus has the power on Earth to forgive sins; it takes power to be saved.

It takes anointing to preach the Word to the sinner or the seeker who desires to be saved. It takes anointing for the listener to be able to hear the Word. It takes an anointing for the listener to *receive* the Word and hide it in his heart.

If you have a heart for souls and you do the work of an evangelist – as you should, you should fast for those whom you are standing in the gap for to receive salvation. It you are going out to witness, you should be fasted. A prophetess told me if you really want your prayers heard, then fast.

Touch not God's anointed. Touch not god's anoint*ing*. There is the five-fold ministry anointing. Apostolic anointing, Prophetic anointing. Soul winners anointing. Missionary anointing. Teaching and Bible exposition anointing. Pastoral anointing.

There is anointing to minister to others. There is anointing to sing, for example. Some people have that anointing, and some don't. However, we do not judge the joyful songs or joyful noise that others bring unto the Lord. Those songs are to God and not to us. There is a musician's anointing, as well the anointing to preach the Word of God. Preaching is not theatrics, it is presenting the Word, preaching Christ and Him crucified, not entertaining people.

Whatever God has appointed you to do, He's anointed you to do. Every gift is very important. One gift is not more important than the other.

There are anointings for those who are to be a support to the Gospel. Some of those supporters have the financial dominion anointing. *Whoa, whoa, whoa.* People keep praying for finances and money – seems there is an anointing or a level of anointing for that.

DO NOT SEEK THE TREASURE, instead ask for the **anointing,** not the money. That would be the difference between being given a fish or being taught how to fish. Ask for the anointing. Prepare yourself to receive the anointing. Be faithful—very faithful in the small things so that the true riches will be entrusted to you. We don't seek the money, we seek the *anointing*. That is especially important because if you don't have the anointing or the empowerment, you will seek in vain.

Additionally, I am quite fond of the writers anointing; thank You, Lord.

There are many gifts of the Spirit and they come from the same Spirit, the Holy Spirit, but there are different administrations of each gift. Intercessors have an anointing, while deliverance pastors and ministers have the deliverance anointing. A person can have multiple gifts. Some have the anointing for the Gifts of Healing, and others may flow under an anointing for creativity and invention. Witty ideas and new inventions come from the LORD.

And very important is the Administrative anointing. But so many people want to be in charge. To do so, they need a Leadership anointing. People want to be the boss, but if you don't have an anointing for it, you either won't be, you won't be successful at it, that is, people won't honor your leadership and follow you.

On this list of types of anointings is the counseling anointing which is a very beautiful gift. **God anoints everything that needs anointing**. God anoints everything that He deals with to empower it and make it alive to thrive. There is an anointing to be a wife. There is an anointing to be a husband. There is an anointing to be a parent.

All of these anointings are important and valuable. All are needed in the Body of Christ for a body to be fitly joined together and functioning as God intended.

No one should think the anointing of another is disposable, but their own anointing is not, when all godly anointing comes from God. All is necessary, powerful, and is working a purpose in the Earth. And, since it is from God, it is precious.

If anointing were diamonds, we could easily see it's worth.

> "*It is* like the precious ointment upon the head, that ran down upon the beard, *even* Aaron's beard: that went down to the skirts of his garments;
> (Psalms 133:2)

Anything that God is giving out, or pouring out is precious; anything from the Hand of God, especially when it crosses the interface from the spiritual to the natural, it is precious. Recall the Israelites were fed manna in the Wilderness – God gave it out a certain way and it was to be used a certain way.

People? Americans?--, think that rules and instructions are optional? They are not. We do what God says do with what God gives out.

What anointing you receive is for your purpose and your destiny. It is not just so you can have an anointing. You have anointing for a purpose. Anointing is empowerment.

Think of yourself as a beautiful house. Imagine any kind of house you like. You are lovely, but you are just sitting there in a lovely setting. Anointing is like the electricity to that house, the lights come on--, now you can see. Now you can see what you're doing and now you can plug things in (appliances) to power them, get them running so you can accomplish things.

Anointing is attractive. It always has been, and it always will be. Anointing is attractive because people, they especially say women are drawn to power. I say everyone is drawn to power. Money is power; people are drawn to it. Powerful people draw people, that's why they follow them and vote for them.

Anointing is powerful, especially when it is of God because God is the greatest power, therefore His anointing would be most attractive. The soul winner's anointing, for example, should draw seekers and the lost. It's supposed to.

God's anointing is also attractive to the enemy, he runs to it, he wants it; he can't get it from God so he tries to steal it from man who may not know it's value, or even that he has it. Further, many do not know how to guard or protect the anointing. Yes, the anointing is protecting you, but you need to be wise with the anointing God entrusts to you.

Anointing is attractive. It is how so many pastors and preachers get into so much trouble. Yes, they are mishandling anointing and folks are drawn to the anointing, but they and the preacher may think that they themselves are the object of another's desire. Again, it could be the enemy in the soul of the person who is chasing a pastor, or a music minister, or in the world, even a famous or rich celebrity.

Once a person is anointed, they are of more interest to everyone because even the enemy is drawn to anointing.

People want power; it is why folks practice witchcraft, for example. People want things to happen when they speak. People want their way. People want comfort, money and the "good life." Most often people who delve into witchcraft and other sins do so until they find another power that is greater than the one they are serving.

God is the Highest Power and He will never be defeated. But it is up to us as soul winners to present and introduce Jesus to the lost and the seekers. We need anointing for that because we need to introduce the Lord with power, even signs and wonders, else--, it will not draw as it should.

Repent

Many people behave as if they think Destiny is optional – it is not, but this is why people think they can get saved--, check that box off, go back out into the world and live like a son of a gun and wait until the last moment of life to repent and believe they are going right on to Glory, right to Heaven.

I'm not saying that they are not, that's between them and God. But what happened in between since you got saved at 15 and now that you're 100 and knocking on Heaven's door? In that 85 years, what did you do? What have you accomplished? What of your Purpose? What of your Destiny? Do you have anything you can leave to anybody?

What of your Legacy? Have you left your kids in the place you were supposed to leave them so they could start out on *their* Destiny?

Not pursuing and fulfilling destiny is like going to school but never doing any homework. YOU FAIL.

Please don't fail.

God's going to be checking for this.

Your boss at work asks to see your files and folders at the end of the week to see if you're doing what you were hired for or assigned to do.

God will be checking for this. That is one of the reasons why there will be a judgment--, it is to judge <u>your works</u>. A lot of preachers have taught that judgement is to judge if you were saved or not so you can get into Heaven. Okay --, but if you get into Heaven, at what level? That's why all of us need good works, even though we are not saved by works, but by faith and by the Grace of God, salvation is a gift. But our Christian works will be tried with FIRE. If they are hay, wood, or stubble, they will burn. Our works need to be solid and real, like gold so in the Fire we will not be deedless. If we reach destiny, our fullest potential spiritually, are deeds are all assured.

Do we think that what we want is more important than what God wants? Do we dare? Do we even dare to ignore our own destiny?

Do we even dare to try to mess with other people's destiny?

Saul wanted to KILL David – Saul decided that David should be killed because what God put in David *wasn't important*? Wasn't necessary? Wasn't *of* God? Did Saul even give this a thought? How did Saul even come up with this idea? Saul made a demonic decision.

Anyone who wants to **kill** another is planning to touch the plan of God. They are planning to touch another person's destiny. They are intending to undo the plan of God.

- Cain against Abel.
- Joseph's brothers, against Joseph.
- Pharoah against all the Hebrews who were trying to escape Egypt.

Have you thought about or practiced what you're going to say to God when He asks you why you didn't fulfill **your Destiny**, or even try?

What will you say? *I got saved, but then I went to college and then I was partying for 85 years, and suddenly I was 100 years old, and I don't know where the time went.* Folks, you know that's not a good answer.

We don't know how long it will take to repent, so don't waste 85 years <u>not</u>

repenting, and especially living like a son of a gun and adding things to the list of things that you need to repent for. It is good that man always repents. Repent every day, especially if you are not seriously pursuing **destiny**. Repent if you have dared touch or interfere with the anointing, or the *destiny* of another person.

Uzzah

Uzzah touched the Ark of the Covenant. Just because anointing is not in a gold box with angel wings on it, it doesn't mean that it's not precious. God places more value on a man than on a gold box with carvings.

Uzzah touched the Ark of the Covenant and was killed. That right there is why we don't touch what God says don't touch. Do not touch anointed things that you have no business touching; do not touch God's anointing.

Most of us think that we are not supposed to touch God. Yes, that is true; Uzzah died when he touched the Ark of the Covenant. It also means we don't touch the *anointing* in another soul. Says God, not me.

The woman with the precious ointment who anointed Jesus' feet, had what was precious in a precious alabaster box. I believe that is how God sees us, His precious people in which He puts His precious anointing. Everything God gives a man is anointed, and that includes Destiny.

If God does not anoint the things that He gives a man, then it will not be empowered; it would be dead. We also know that God doesn't deal with dead things. He doesn't make dead things. God quickens the dead; He makes alive. Things made with man's hands are not made alive by man or by God; those things are idols. Idols are considered dead and dumb. Let's put it this way, if God is not enlivening them, even though they may find a way to become animated, they are still spiritually dead things.

He Knew Us

I repeat: touch not God's anointed. Touch not God's anointing. Do His prophet no harm. We each have a God-given destiny. God knew us when we were in our mother's wombs. He wrote about the days fashioned for us and their number in His Book. As Jesus said, I come in the volume of the Book it is written of Me. God knows it all, what gifts we have, how long we will live, our Kingdom purpose, as well as our Destiny.

God anoints it because in the Earth we need **power** to overcome the natural power in the Earth, the prince of this world. We need anointing and empowerment to **overcome** what is going to come up against us.

Destiny is anointed.

But there are too many who only want what they want and do not give a care as to what God says. Some of these folks may realize and know that they have anointing and then try to subvert that anointing to another use, usually selfish use, entirely.

That is rebellion, and rebellion is as the sin of witchcraft. Too many take spiritual gifts given by God and misuse them on the dark side instead of for the Kingdom.

Those things will not end well.

Whose *Will*?

My God – there should not be this much witchcraft in the world, should there? But there is.

There should be **NO** witchcraft in the church, but there is.

Do we dare think that what we want is more important than what God has planned and what God wants? Do we dare? How many singers brag that they got their singing gift from God? How many were brought up in the church but now they are singing R&B and other secular genres? Did God say they could leave the church, or did Mammon call?

I've been married before – and while going through that divorce I prayed and prayed and prayed asking God for what *I* wanted – then one day I realized that if I'm praying to God and my saved, estranged husband is praying to God, then why are we praying two entirely different things, even two opposing things, two opposite things? So, I **STOPPED** praying with the understanding that day and only prayed in the Spirit because that's what the Holy Spirit led me to do. I only prayed in the Spirit because I did not want to pray anything ungodly.

Divorce is rough, but it shouldn't be a battle to the death as if the couple has turned into gladiators in the Roman Coliseum. Sometimes God requires us to shut our mouths. I thank God that the Holy Spirit instructed me to do that.

Now, who "won" in that divorce?

Ask God.

Not Interchangeable

Now I will present a couple of scenarios from the Bible.

Zechariah was married to Elizabeth, and she was with child, John the Baptist – one of my favorites.

Mary was overshadowed by the Holy Spirit and was with child. Joseph was Jesus' father. Mary had Jesus of Nazareth.

Does anyone reading this book think that either of those two couples were *optional, random, or interchangeable*? Does anybody think that **any** two could come together to have either John the Baptist, or Jesus of Nazareth?

The world thinks like that. The world thinks and operates on the premise that destiny, marriages, and children are random, optional, or whoever gets there first is a thing. The world plans their marriages, lives and children by the flesh. They plan by their comfort, flesh desires and how cute they want their kids to be. That's why there is so much drama in relationships in the world; this shouldn't be in the Church. That's why there is so much competition and fighting and sin and divorces, in the world. Church, please stop behaving this way. In olden days, the parents selected the marriage partner for their child.

Shall we do better and plan spiritually for our relationships, friendships, connections, marriages and even children? Should we ask God, *What do you want me to do? What seed are You planning to bring to the Earth and do I have anything to do with it?*

What do I have to do with it? Who is the spouse You have selected for me?

Nowadays, as in Isaiah, could it be that 7 women are vying for one man. God made someone for everyone--, even the animals. Why are we six men short?

Because we are out of the Plan of God for man and the Earth. Who is out of step? Any number of folks. Pray you aren't one of them. Amen.

Please tell me where is God in those seven women seeking *one* fellow? God has ordained one woman, and it may not even be one of the seven that are fighting over him to be with that man.

Adam, and then Eve, one plus one, it wasn't complicated. Adam didn't look for Eve for 10 years before he found her. Neither of them had to go on a dating show, or fight off two other guys and three, or six other women to finally connect and marry.

Too Much Witchcraft

But just like in the world, this is why there is manipulation, control, domination, lying, & scheming, even in the Church –, either over a man or over a position or a title--, or just attention. This is witchcraft. There is too much witchcraft everywhere and there should be **none** in the Church.

Those who do this kind of witchcraft are either *blind witches* (most are not; they know exactly what they are doing and they think they will get away with it. but if God has put **destiny** in a title, a position, or a relationship then God has given the Grace and the anointing for those who are to be in that position, or in that relationship to know what is going on.

When two women are vying for the same man, whether he knows it or not, this is the beginning of polygamous witchcraft. That man must be with the woman God has chosen for him; is important to both of their destinies.

When two men are vying for the same woman, whether she knows it or not, this is the beginning of polygamous witchcraft. That woman should be with whichever man that God has selected because this is integral to their destiny.

When two people are vying for the same position or title, unless both of them are saved to the utmost, resisting the devil and do not have the witchcraft gene – (which is not really a thing, I made that up) – the witchcraft and games are likely to begin. The competition, the extreme competition starts, and this fosters witchcraft.

Yeah, but we have free will.

Sure, we do. God will have His plan fulfilled in the Earth. Do you want to be part of God's plan, as He has called you to be, or do you want to do your own thing? Happy and prosperous is doing the will of Him who sent you, doing the will of God. Know that God will have His way in the plan for man and the Earth--, if He has to work around you, He will. God is always spiritual, He may have to work around you to fulfill His plan in the Earth.

While you pursue what you think is happiness, or prosperity, or success. If you are pursuing the flesh life God may have to pass you by.

Good luck with that.

There is too much witchcraft in the Church. Any witchcraft in the church is too much.

The Bible says suffer not a witch to live. If a garden is overgrown with weeds you remove the weeds, yes? Suffer not a weed to live is the mantra of gardeners. Are we not put here like Adam and Eve to "dress the garden"?

Witchcraft in people's lives may start out as early as school bullies. At school some older or bigger kids may gang up on a younger one, tease him, call him names, steal his lunch or his lunch money. Power plays, domination, control, and manipulation are all witchcraft. Bullies are either cowards or very strategic. Well, they could be both.

Racism is witchcraft. Anything seeking control, domination, manipulation is witchcraft. Witches are like bullies who most often hide to do their evil. Not always, some witches are bold, but most are occult. This is why you don't see what is happening sometimes until after it hits you.

When someone is wrong or doing wrong, they will often times recruit another or others to do evil with them. Evil spreads, if not stopped it propagates itself, like weeds. More than one bully is a gang up. Their purpose is to bully, but to bully with back up – their goal is to hurt, scare, or oppose someone, usually someone weaker, smaller, trusting, and unsuspecting while they ensure that nothing, no harm comes to themselves.

If they say, Come with us, let us lay wait for blood, let us lurk privily for the innocent without cause.
(Proverbs 1:11)

…don't do it. Do not become their accomplice in their evil escapades. God will judge.

But *Why*?

Why?

In the world, we know why. But this is what I've seen in the church.

Why?

Because I want something the other person has.

Why?

Because I want something the other person is supposed to have.

Because I have no discernment. Because I have no vision, or I don't hear from God clearly, or correctly. So I don't think God has anything for me.

Why?

Because I think God is random, or I don't want to. Because I think destiny doesn't exist, or I can pick the one I want.

Because I think God has no plan in the Earth and for mankind and I can do what I want.

Why?

I don't have any faith.

Why?

Because this guy (or girl) is not important. They certainly aren't as important as I am and what I want.

Why?

Because I have fear that I won't get what the other person is now getting, or the one I may get won't be as good. Yeah—because I have no faith.

Why?

Because I think I can override the plan of God. This is full force rebellion and stone-cold witchcraft.

Why?

Because I really want this position so much.

Why?

Because I really want this title so much.

Why?

Because I really want this man so much. Because I saw him first.

Why?

Because I want to change my own destiny from what God says it is. I might not even know what it is, or that I have a destiny, but I see some options over there that look good. We can just shop for a new destiny, right?

Nope.

So what have I done?

I've stopped praying for the will of God and now I praying my own will – and that is SOULISH PRAYERS.

Why?

Because my salvation is questionable and I behave just like the people in the world.

Because I totally disrespect the anointing, calling, purpose and destiny of the person who's place I want to take – whose life I want to take over—

And if it is a man that I'm trying to get with, I don't respect him or his anointing or destiny either – because if I'm not really a part of his destiny I may mess him completely up – by inserting myself into his life, but I don't care.

Praying soulish prayers and this kind of manipulations confirms the person or persons praying them as a witch or witches (warlocks). This means that the person they want to get with will be getting with a WITCH.

I heard an apostle recently say that if you marry a witch, your destiny is shot; it's over.

So as a witch who wants to manipulate a relationship, you are really sacrificing your Destiny and the object of your desires' Destiny.

Why?

Because I disregard their Destiny and I do not fear GOD—so I don't mind stepping into another's Destiny/LIFE as an imposter and interloper.

Saints of God, there is too much witchcraft in the world. There is too much witchcraft in the Body of Christ. *There is too much witchcraft in the Church. Any* witchcraft is *too much* witchcraft.

Soulish Prayers

Soulish prayers and gang ups can happen, where two or more have decided that they want to accomplish a thing that is not of God. It is evil because it is against God's will, and God's plans, but they don't see it as evil because they've agreed on it. They've voted on it, and struck hands, and even joined hands in prayer. Evil will recruit another or others to join in, just like bullies.

Did the Pharisees, Sadducees or Sanhedrin Council, or the Romans ever ask GOD, *Is Jesus Your Son, for real?* No, they went with the wisdom of men, which is most often demonic and did as they saw fit; they did what seemed right to suit their own selfish needs and maintain their high positions in politics and society.

This is solid abuse of, *Where two or more are gathered,* but people do it all the time.

One can put a thousand to flight, two--, 10,000.

How should one chase a thousand, and
two put ten thousand to flight, except
their Rock had sold them, and the
LORD had shut them up?
(Deuteronomy 32:30)

Later in this book we will compare and contrast and deal with natural gang ups versus spiritual gang-ups. But know that natural gang ups are inspired from the spirit, so you have to pray against both setups to be free.

Two Or More

> If they say, Come with us, let us lay wait for blood, let us lurk privily for the innocent without cause.
> (Proverbs 1:11)

Where two or more are gathered in my name is what the Scripture says. God says, **There will I be in the midst.** Just because you're <u>in</u> a church *building*, or you hold titles within that local church, doesn't mean you've *gathered* in the Lord's Name, that is in His character, reputation, and in His WILL.

> Indeed they shall surely assemble, *but* not because of Me. Whoever assembles against you shall fall for your sake. (Isaiah 54:15-17)

Pharisees were a gang up against Jesus. Sadducees were a gang up also against Jesus. Jesus was profiled. Daily. When Jesus was apprehended, they ganged up on Jesus, but released Barabbas.

People get together in the natural for ungodly reasons all the time. They form cliques, such as pain cliques, or jealousy cliques. Witchcraft forms cliques. There are singular witches, but most prefer to be in a coven. There are competition cliques where someone may be competing with someone who is not even competing with them.

I don't respect bullies, but at least a bully is out there in the open, while an unfriendly friend is sneaking, hiding--, like a witch. Witchcraft only works if there is a person close enough to you to be a devil agent to do you harm.

I've just introduced the Unfriendly Friend (also designated as UF in this book).

The Unfriendly Friend

The unfriendly friend in Jesus' life, of course, was Judas.

A person who pretends to be your friend, but is not, is an unfriendly friend, or a frenemy. This pretense is not necessarily short term; it could last days, weeks, months, years, or an entire lifetime. There was a woman who had dated a married man for 17 years. This man's wife was that side hen—she was way too old to be a chick; she was up in age--, a hen. She was the "best friend" to the cheating man's **wife**!

Yeah, with *friends* like that, the woman's husband doesn't have to go out in the streets. Sin was delivered to his doorstep. So-called friends may destroy each other, but there is a real friend that sticks closer than a brother, Proverbs 18:24.

The unfriendly friend is an enemy in masquerade. He or she is a backstabber, backbiter, traitor, and betrayer, (Luke 21:6). This unfriendly friend is close enough to really betray you. This UF will conspire with others and gang up on a person who trusts them with secrets and with information of a sensitive nature.

Oh, bless your heart they may say, and they don't mean it in a good way, but sarcastically. You think they mean you well--, and they may even say that they do. But, they don't. They are jealous, covetous, evil and sneaky. They may have nice things, but they don't want you to have nice things, blessings and successes. They have a number of *spirits*, surely, but an *emptier spirit* comes to mind.

Most of all, the UF has a secret agenda in this relationship which is not of God, and it has nothing to do with what God says or expects the outcome to be. Their agenda is either their own—all their own, or it is inspired by others who hate this unsuspecting friend, and ultimately the root source is the devil.

Joseph's 10 older brothers were unfriendly friends. They were so oppressed by the devil that they were willing to try to destroy the anointed Destiny of another, even their own brother.

Normally, Destiny hunters and killers are witches, warlocks, and wizards, but these brothers stepped right up to do evil. Touch not mine anointed, do My prophet no harm. Before you set out to attack, steal from or do harm to anyone you'd better ask God, *Who is that person to You?* God has a hedge of protection around His prophet. You want to break that hedge? Don't. The Serpent of the Lord lays beyond that hedge and he who breaks that hedge will be bitten.

> He that diggeth a pit shall fall into it;
> and whoso breaketh an hedge, a
> serpent shall bite him.
> (Ecclesiastes 10:8)

Pride & the Fake Friend

An unfriendly friend can wreck a life. An unfriendly friend can wreck a plan, a blessing, even a ministry. Look at Jesus--, if Jesus had not been Jesus, Judas could have brought that ministry down. If Jesus hadn't trained 11 other Disciples who would later become Apostles and keep the ministry going, Judas could have torn Jesus' ministry down.

An unfriendly friend can serve in any position in your life, and even in a church. An UF is usually full of pride. In their heart they may be asking, *Who do you think you are,* when they are the one full of themselves. They may be thinking all kinds of evil thoughts such as you must think you are so much, or you think you are cute. All the while if you are in God you may not be thinking any of that. You are not insecure and weak, but you are not so narcissistic and self-focused as they probably are.

As it pertains to the case that they may have invented against you, this person is full of pride, and they have to be right with all of their accusations against you. Some have something to prove, or think they have something to prove. For example, they could have *propha-lied* to someone telling them that man (whoever that man is) is the future husband of the person they are talking to.

This is not true because they did not hear from God and because of all their demons, they really don't even hear from God. Anyway, they've *proph-a-lied* and now will do everything in their power not to be caught in a lie. This man becoming the husband of their other friend, as loosely as any friendship is with them--- is not in the plan of God or in the destiny of any of the people that your UF wants to matchmake.

They may not have even said, *Thus saith the Lord*; they just decided themselves or among the two in the gang that they would manipulate this man to a wedding altar and sacrifice his Destiny of the altar of *I-Don't-Really-Care About Your-Destiny-But-I-Really-Want-To-Get-Married*.

Folks, you corner a narcissist, a *propha-liar*, or an unfriendly friend, you've got a snake on your hands. These folks will go through great pains to **prove** that they were not lying and that they are right--, here comes the flesh, and here comes the witchcraft.

- God of Heaven, deny the prayers of the enemies of my Destiny, in the Name of Jesus.

- God of Heaven do not let my enemies hide behind angels or the Word of God, in the Name of Jesus.
- God of Heaven, break any shield around them and arrest them, convict them, and if they do not repent, let their powers DIE, in the Name of Jesus.
- Father, as You did for Moses, do no let any enemy snake be greater than the Lord's Fiery Serpent, in the Name of Jesus.

An evil friend, just like the devil has nothing but evil plans against others. They have convinced themselves that they are ok, and their "friend" is the problem. They have convinced themselves that they are clever, and they are "keeping their enemy close." But sadly, they are the enemy, not the unsuspecting friend. An UF hates you, but don't marvel at that--, they probably hate everyone. They may be jealous of everyone. They are mercurial and usually can't be trusted, but somehow they or the devil has convinced you that it's you and you are not kind enough, or patient enough, or too mistrusting.

Repent anyway, but it's most likely not you that's the problem. Repentance can never hurt you. But, never shut down the Holy Spirit when He is telling you something important, such as who a character is.

And finally, to prove their "rightness" this UF begins to circulate your name around for evil. In the natural, they must do this because that's what UF's and narcissists do. It's so if they get jammed up, they've already maligned your name, so your credibility is shot. That's if they dare; and most do.

In the spiritual realms, oh yeah, they will put your name out there for sure. Gang ups do physical things to others, but spiritual gang ups are those who are praying soulish prayers, either as *blind witches* or actual, practicing witches –, even in the Church.

If you know or think you know who is practicing witchcraft against you, and you think there's only one UF – don't be deceived. If you think there are only two of them, don't be deceived. Remember, these are witches, and a coven is 13. Thirteen means they can incant 24 hours a day. Just because a person is a *blind witch*, they may not know that they go to the coven at night. If they are practicing witchcraft, they are a witch. Period. If they are practicing witchcraft the devil knows it because they are calling on his powers. And, the coven knows it, even if the blind witch doesn't because they go there at night, but their "dreams" are wiped.

So, you'd better get prayed up and stay prayed up if there's a bully, a witch, or a gang up against you, in the Name of Jesus.

Lord, put a sword, Your fiery, Flaming Sword between and every fake friend coming against me for affliction, or worse with their gang up prayers, their witchcraft prayers, their soulish prayers and selfish *I-wants*, in the Name of Jesus.

First thing, send all those arrows Back to Sender, sevenfold, in the Name of Jesus.

- Lord, remove all protection from anyone who is coming against Your anointing and purpose, for my life, in the Name of Jesus.

Lord, remove all protection from anyone who has or is attempting to tamper with my Destiny. Expose them, Lord; expose them, in Jesus' Name.

I bind up all enemy reinforcements and counterattacks in the Name of Jesus.

Prayers Against Unfriendly Friends

Holy Spirit, incubate me with Your Fire, in the Name of Jesus.

Holy Spirit, incubate my life with Your Fire, in the Name of Jesus.

My life, receive Fire, become Fire, in the Name of Jesus. (X5)

Fire of God, deliver me now, in the Name of Jesus.

Every battle in my life that is raging out of envy, jealousy, competition, excessive competition, or pettiness, scatter by Fire, scatter by Fire, in the Name of Jesus.

Blood of Jesus, close all enemy access points into my life, in Jesus' Name.

Every harm done against me using my pictures or anything that represents me, burn to ashes, spontaneously, in the Name of Jesus.

Wherever my name is being called for evil, Holy Ghost Fire, answer for me, in the Name of Jesus.

Wherever my name is being called for evil, Blood of Jesus, answer for me, in the Name of Jesus.

Blood of Jesus, separate me from all fake friends, in the Name of Jesus.

Holy Ghost Fire, chase away every unfriendly friend in my life, in the Name of Jesus.

Every power that has dug a pit for me, fall into your own pit and die, and I shall escape unharmed, in the Name of Jesus.

Powers circulating my name for evil, your time is up, die, in the Name of Jesus.

I break and dismantle every evil curse, every incantation, hex, or vex, in the Name of Jesus.

Yoke-breaking anointing fall on my life now, in the Name of Jesus. (X2)

Every attack of envious enemies, especially gang ups, I command you to fail against me, in the Name of Jesus.

Sword of Fire, cut off every evil attachment in my life, in Jesus' Name.

Blood of Jesus (X7) separate my life and Destiny from every unfriendly friend, in the Name of Jesus.

Power in the Blood of Jesus, protect my Destiny from manipulation by any household witch, unfriendly friend, or unknown manipulator, in the Name of Jesus.

Sword of Fire, cut off every evil attachment in my life, in the Name of Jesus.

Holy Ghost Fire, purge my life, in the Name of Jesus. (X3)

Every tree the Father did not plant in my life, be cut down, uprooted, and burned to ashes, in Jesus' Name.

Every evil covenant and evil soul tie in my life, break and die, in the Name of Jesus. (X3)

My life, receive Fire, become Fire, in the Name of Jesus. (X3)

Fire of God, deliver me now, in the Name of Jesus. (X3)

My life, receive Fire, become Fire, in the Name of Jesus. (X4).

I command all curses spoken by unfriendly friends over me to break by the power in the Blood of Jesus, in the Name of Jesus.

Holy Spirit, wipe the memory of every evil associate and unfriendly friend of any secret I've ever shared with them that they are now using against me, in the Name of Jesus.

Holy Spirit protect the ears of those who must hear the lies of unfriendly friends speaking against me, and let them not hear or remember what the UF says, in the Name of Jesus.

I fire back, sevenfold every evil arrow of envious witchcraft, polygamous witchcraft, evil associate's witchcraft, and I do not miss my targets, in the Name of Jesus.

Lord, let the stones rolled for my sake, roll back on the rollers of those stones, in the Name of Jesus.

Anything taken from me that is on any evil altar, I separate myself from you and I command you to catch Fire, catch Fire, catch Fire, in the Name of Jesus.

Every evil load transferred into my life by unfriendly friends, you have a delivery--, I've sent your entire evil load back to you, in the Name of Jesus.

I dismantle every evil yoke of unfriendly friends, in the Name of Jesus.

Thank You, Lord for delivering me from the grip of unfriendly friends, in the Name of Jesus.

* Prayers Against Unfriendly Friends adapted or inspired by Pastor Teddy Omozegbai from his blog: deliverancefireministry.blogspot.com

Goodbye Gang Ups

God handled gangs in the Bible.

Lord, in the Name of Jesus what you did in the Bible for gang ups do it for me in the natural. Lord, natural or spiritual gang ups, let them be scattered, in the Name of Jesus.

> So he prepared a large festival for them, and when they had finished eating and drinking, he sent them back to their master, and marauding gangs of Arameans never came into the territory of Israel again.
> (2 Kgs 6:23)

Lord, as you did for Thebes in Ezekiel 30:15, eliminate the gangs and the gang ups against Your darling, in the Name of Jesus.

I'll pour out my anger on Sin, Egypt's strong fortress, and I'll eliminate the gangs in Thebes. (Ezekiel 30:15)

Gangs as an Egyptian construct were also handled by the Lord.

"Son of Man, tell this to Pharaoh, king of Egypt and his gangs: "Who do you think you are? What makes you so great? (Ezekiel 31:2)

I'm going to make your gangs (and gang ups) die using the weapons of valiant warriors, all of whom are ruthless people. "They will devastate the majesty of Egypt, destroying all of its hordes. (Ezekiel 32:12)

I'm going to make your gang ups die, says the Lord, they will devastate the majesty of Egypt.

If thieves came against you, if marauding gangs by night Oh, how you will be destroyed! Would they not steal only until they had enough? If grape pickers came to you, would they not leave some grapes to be gleaned? (Obadiah 1:5)

Gangs and gang up come to steal, kill & destroy; they are demonic.

Stay prayed up, saints of God.

A Mob & Serpents

Two or more is a gang.

More than a few is a mob. When many gang up on you, in the natural, it may feel overwhelming, but know that the Lord is on your side. When there is a spiritual gang up, if it is not dealt with it will eventually manifest in the natural.

And there was one named Barabbas, which lay bound with them that had made insurrection with him who had committed murder in the insurrection. (Mark 15:7)

But the chief priests moved the people, that he should rather release Barabbas unto them. (Mark 15:11)

And so Pilate, willing to content the people, released Barabbas unto them, and delivered Jesus, when he had

scourged him, to be crucified.
(Mark 15:15)

Gathered before Pilate, was a gang up, a mob against Jesus that wanted Barabbas instead of Jesus. The Pharisees finally had incited the people to gang up on Jesus and they cried for Jesus to be crucified and to let the robber go free.

Give us Barabbas was the chant.

I say all this to remind us that after the passion of the Christ and the mob mentality had left the people and the crucifixion had happened: they went away sorrowful (Matthew 19).

There is an evil anointing on evil prayers. Those powers infiltrate the prayers and those who are praying them. For the evil that they intend to cause to come to pass there must be an evil anointing.

But later, as cooler heads prevail, those who invoked that evil will be sorrowful. Wasn't Judas immediately sorrowful after he had betrayed Jesus? Betraying the Godly may lead to a moment of celebration, but eventually the counterfeit blessing promised by the devil is snatched away and the devil rejoices because he got two with one stone: the betrayer and the betrayed.

The blessing of the Lord brings no sorrow, but the counter is the result of the devils' "blessings." Take time to consider that please.

The devil has power. It doesn't rival God's power, but it can rival the power of an ignorant, selfish, or desperate man, because a man who doesn't know who he is will not use the power he has properly, or at all. The warning here is that devil anointing takes over in soulish prayers, and then you will need the Spirit of God to override demons called up from the pit of hell. Those demons are *loosed* to do the will of the devil when a person is speaking or praying something ungodly, from soulish prayers to outright curses.

Even if you blindly or mistakenly do this, once you do it, you fall from your position of authority over them, you are no longer in position with God to deal with these demons. Your ability to put 1,000 or 10,000 to flight with God is diminished or gone when you have defected to the dark side.

That works on both sides, you know. So, if you have called up 1,000 demons, how do you expect to handle them?

No matter who you think you are in a coven, you can't manage them when they get out of hand, and they will get out of hand. Who do you think you are is what was asked of Pharaoh. Those who are seeking affliction or death on another are operating under a *pharaoh spirit*. Pharaoh only understands and responds to Death. But later when things get out of control when you are out of position with God and rendered weak and/or powerless, what are you going to do? My question is, do they get out of hand because they know you have fallen either to their level, or lower so they don't fear you anymore, or do they gang up on the one who called them to gang up on another person? Sow and reap?

Saints of God, the only way and reason they don't take over that person is because that person starts to feed them. They feed on worship and that includes sacrifices of others that they can oppress, overwhelm, or take out. It's very much like the criminal system in the natural where deals are made, Mr. So & So can go free if he *"gives them"* someone else. In the demonic world I don't think they need a bigger fish, as when the Vice Squad of the Police let a small fish go, if they help them get the kingpin of a drug operation, for example.

In the dark kingdom, maybe just a fish, or several fish will do to save the life of the person praying soulish and demonic prayers to fulfill their own personal lusts-- today. But if successful, these demons will call again for more sacrifice.

You may have seen this where a person is a nobody until a few members of their family suddenly die, then all of a sudden, the one secretly praying evil prayers becomes a famous, rich, celebrity.

This is not a one-time thing; the devil makes generational covenants to be able to decimate an entire bloodline, not just one person at a time. Consider soberly what happens to people around the people you know and deal with. If there is a lot of death---, you'd better run. And be sure to stay prayed up while you are running away!

Spiritually speaking you will not be able to do what you normally would because you cavorted with those demonic *spirits*. The only reason they don't take out the one who called them is because that one is turning over others as sacrifices. Saints of God, you'd better stay prayed up and discern who you are dealing with in this life.

Guard your words, guard your thoughts, guard your prayer life. Guard your lust, wishes and desires so you are not blindly cursing anyone or wishing evil on people. Respect God and His anointing, no matter who it's in. Respect God's purpose in you and in others. Do not disrespect God's anointed; do His prophet no harm. **Do not *try* to do God's prophet's harm because in order to do that you will be calling on demons and when they cannot take out God's** prophet, what you asked for will fall on your head.

Touch not God's anointed and do His prophet no harm. That Scripture is for the protection of the person who would even try such a thing. When you are trying to hurt God's Prophet, you are hurting yourself. I repeat for emphasis that God has a hedge of protection around His Prophet because that Prophet is anointed. You want to break that hedge in order to attack a prophet that you only see as a man or a woman? The Serpent of the Lord lays beyond that hedge and he who breaks that hedge will be bitten.

> He that diggeth a pit shall fall into it; and whoso breaketh an hedge, a serpent shall bite him.
> (Ecclesiastes 10:8)

No matter what you want, **ask God first** – *God, is this for me*? If a thing, position, relationship is not for you and/or not for you in this season, don't ask for it. Blindly, you could be praying satanic and soulish prayers asking for something you have no business having. In that case you could call up all kinds of hell into your own life.

No matter how many of you there are and what evil you may have agreed to, God is greater, His anointing is greater, His anointed one is greater, and His fiery serpents don't miss.

> And the LORD sent fiery serpents among the people, and they bit the people; and much people of Israel died. (Numbers 21:6)

Why Gang Ups

Gang ups are not just bullies and unfriendly friends in the natural; it starts in the spirit. Some may not have awareness that they are being ganged up on or attacked in a serial or constant manner. Some do. But if you are one to always feel threatened, attacked, weary, worried, you may be under spiritual gang up that hasn't manifested in the natural, yet. If you wake up exhausted every morning where you've slept enough hours to not be exhausted, you may be under this kind of attack. If you are attacked, chased, or pursued often in your dreams, your prayer life needs to be stepped up and you may need to seek deliverance from this. Some dream attacks that seem so real may be evil human agents astral projecting into your home, bedroom, or life. There should not be witchcraft in the Church, but I know of at least one "pastor" who does this. I know because he did it to me. Do I think there's only one? *Oh please.*

Almost anyone who is into witchcraft can gang up and stalk or attack you--, even your own family members. These people decide what they are going to do in the daytime in their thoughts, words, and prayers.

What makes them do this? Jealousy. Lust. Revenge, or any work of the flesh. In so doing they become evil human agents who are either seeking to assault your body, sell your soul, block your blessings by stealing from you, and/or kill or destroy thereby rendering a sacrifice to the devil whether they realize that's what they were doing, or not.

Didn't Jesus say, **If you are not for Me, you are against Me?** (Matthew 12:30). If any part, especially any *anointed* part of you or your life is being sacrificed or someone is trying to sacrifice it, the one doing the evil is either knowingly or unknowingly trying to save their own life, and /or receive promotion in the dark kingdom.

This is no different than a gang member or would-be gang member going out to commit murder to be jumped into a gang or to be promoted within the ranks of that gang.

The reason people in the natural act just like spiritual gang ups and spiritual gang stalkers is because they have been overcome and invaded, inhabited by those evil *spirits*. Then, they took on the nature of those *spirits*. I don't mean recently took on the nature of evil demons. A person could have been this way since before they were saved, but pretended to be nice but still carrying around those evil *spirits*. Then one day the nature of those evil entities surfaced.

One may have said, *I wish thus and so*.

The other may have said, *You know, I feel the same way.*

Well, they both just invited some demons who want to steal, kill, and destroy. Maybe they feel good that they have a friend, a buddy who agrees with them and sees it the way they see it. One may even feel "loved" because someone cares about their feelings and wants. *Someone finally understands my feelings and feels the way I do*, they may think or say.

Those are real feelings, but there is a demonic anointing to all of them. Everything you feel and experience that is spiritual is not necessarily of God. The devil is a great pretender, a great counterfeiter and deceiver. Just because a thing feels spiritual doesn't mean it is of God.

The devil has anointing. That anointing makes things feel spiritual.

The devil gives out anointing.

It takes anointing to sin.

People of God, when others are praying ungodly, soulish prayers, even in the church--, or Church-adjacent, they are invoking demons to do the ungodly. There is no angel of God who will work against the Word of God. There is no angel of God who will work against the Plan of God. There is no angel of God who will work against what God has anointed. A man's destiny is anointed. Your destiny is anointed. Anyone who wants to sacrifice it or diminish or banish you with it is of the devil. Therefore, they do not have God or His angels on their side, they have called up demons. When they or anyone is asking for something that is not the will of God, they have made evil contracts and devil deals, and someone will have to pay sooner or later. Be sure you are not the one paying for the devil deal that you know nothing (or little) about and that you did not benefit from.

In gang ups, these people, although they agree with one another, although they've voted on it and are tickled with their plan and think they will get away with it--, they will not.

Even though they think they will be so happy if what they are praying about comes to pass. They will not. Not in the long run. Soulish and satanic prayers invoke demons, and the invokers will have to **PAY** those demons, sooner or later. Further, these are counterfeit promises made by devils. If it is a position or title promised, they will suffer in it. If it is a relationship, it will suffer because it is not of God and God is not in it. It has, instead, been masterminded and orchestrated, and manipulated by humans or demon-driven humans. The people in that relationship will suffer when it is not of God, and they are not with their correct Destiny spouses.

Demonic "love" is not real love. Only God has and gives real love. Man does not have love of his own, it must be given by GOD.

Could this be why there are so many divorces in the world, and even in the Church?

Prayers Against Gang Ups

The following is a prayer against gang ups, and mobs. It has been adapted from Bride Movement (Dan Duval) but there are some changes in it. You can see the full original prayer on the Bride Movement website.

As a start, be sure you are Protestant saved, have repented to God, and confessed your sins before you pray this prayer, or any prayer that I recommend to you. Else, your situation could get worse rather than better. Any good prayer you get, pray it often until you get deliverance, or release to stop praying that particular prayer.

Father, in Heaven, I come before You in the mighty Name of Jesus Christ and I declare that Your Word says I can come boldly before Your Throne of Grace to find Mercy and Grace to help in time of need.

Lord, I have been pursued by unfriendly friends, fake friends, and enemies which lay claim to my God-ordained position, my Destiny and even my life. I know they are not playing with me. Plus, as demons have been invoked, these evil pray-*ers* have no control over the demons that they've loosed out of hell.

Lord, deliver me from the evil man. Deliver me from the deceived man. Lord, protect me from the ignorance of greedy, lustful, self-willed man, in the Name of Jesus.

Lord, I am seeking a judgment in the Courts of Heaven, in my favor, that will empower me to walk out of this wickedness, in Christ Jesus.

Father, I call for a Court to be set, and I petition Jesus Christ to provide the angels of the Lord with the coordinates of my enemies which are pursuing me to destroy me, to cause me to turn from Your Truth, to try to control me, detour me, or devour me, so they can steal, kill, or destroy or take what I have, or what I am to have *IN YOU*.

Lord, I pray that the angels of the Lord would use the Net of the Lord, and any other weapons and technologies necessary, to capture those that pursue me. I call them indicted, and I summon them into the Court of Heaven now, in the Name of Jesus.

(Pause here so those that you have summoned are brought into the Court. After you perceive that they have been brought in, then continue.)

I ask that all hidden documents, covenants, contracts, agreements, certificates, oaths, and vows that have been signed by me or any part of me, including what I will henceforth identify as "the group": clones, holograms, merfolk, twins, copies, duplicates, replicas, derivatives, walk-ins, parents, spouse(s), or ancestors assigning legal rights to those that persecute me, be produced for the Court now.

I call for them to be weighed in the scales of justice.

I invalidate every binding document that has been fraudulently created or established against me based on agreements obtained by me or any part of me or "the group" under duress.

I furthermore invalidate every binding document implicating me or any part of me or "the group" executed by lying spirits that did not fulfill their end of the bargain.

I repent for and renounce the creation of all other documents that are left on behalf of me, my parts, and "the group."

I now call for the Blood of Jesus to stamp every document that has been before the Court empowering those that pursue and persecute me.

I call for them to be nailed to the Cross of Jesus Christ and to be burned in His Consuming Fire.

I call for all of the following elements that have been used as access points to my life in both the natural and the spirit to be presented before the Court and subsequently burned with the Fire of God: hair, fingernails, blood samples, saliva, other sources of DNA, cursed objects, fecal matter, urine, evil sacred trees, ritual altars, covenantal rings, heirlooms, tracking devices, tridents, consent forms, and technologies.

I agree to specifically address anything else that You require of me, Holy Spirit, that would otherwise keep me bound to this persecution. Bring to the front of my mind any specific agreements or sins I need to lay down now, in the Name of Jesus.

Holy Spirit, I confess all my sins, I repent of every sin, and I renounce and denounce every sin and every evil covenant made because of my sin.

All parts of my humanity which allowed any of these attacks against me, I forgive and ask for forgiveness, and repent. Blood of Jesus, you are my defense and I plead for remission of sin and expungement of all iniquity, in the Name of Jesus.

To those that have been summoned into the Court, I declare that my season of persecution at your hands is now over (X3).

It is written that as a man sows, so shall he reap.

It is written that whoever destroys this temple, the Lord will destroy that person. All who have gathered against me but not by the Lord, I shall condemn. I condemn you, I condemn your plots, plans, and schemes against me, my purpose, my future, my destiny, my legacy, my successes and blessings, my relationships and any other good thing the Lord God has planned for me, in the Name of Jesus.

Spiritual entities on assignment by the words, decrees, declarations, incantations, hexes, vexes, soulish prayers, and witchcraft of blind witches, or knowing witches, or deceived Christians, so-called Christians, fake Christians, fake friends, you are FIRED as it concerns me, by the power in the Blood of Jesus, in the Name of Jesus.

I now separate human and partial-human agents from non-human agents within the Court.

To the human and partial-human agents, I offer the Gospel of Jesus Christ. Jesus Christ is the Son of God, Our Creator. He is the firstborn among many brethren. He was born of a virgin, He died for our sins, and was raised again to life on the third day.

He has ascended on high where He is seated at the right hand of the Father and ever lives to make intercession for the saints. He is the payment for our sins, and should you choose Him, you will be justified freely by Grace through the redemption that is found in Him. His suffering will atone for your sins. If you do not choose Him, you will receive in your own members the judgement for your sins and impropriety.

Choose now.

I pray Lord God, that as they make their decisions, Your stream of Living Water flows through the Courtroom to separate out humanity from those that exist as composite entities.

I pray that Your Sword would sever devices, demons, blinders, artificial intelligence, programs, holographic technologies, quantum interfaces, and other defilements that would otherwise inhibit a decision for Jesus to be made by those present in the Court, thus revealing the true conviction of their humanity and not the instruments of their bondage.

Lord, I ask for Your Mercy for myself, and I plead the Blood of Jesus, and I appeal to You to judge and judge justly, and to have Your angels escort those that have not chosen Jesus and all non-human agents to the place determined for them, such that they cannot any longer take or receive assignments against me to destroy my life and deviate me from my heavenly mandates.

Lord, I further implore that they will not be able to influence those who know me, know of me, or are in contact with me in any way to create gang ups against me, be a fake friend to me, or in any way work against my Godly purpose, destiny, connections, relationships, career, family, or ministry, in the Name of Jesus.

I furthermore establish an automation on my freedom such that every reset, regrouping, reinforcement, and retaliation is overcome in accordance with this judgment.

In this, I declare complete freedom and autonomy for my body (respiratory system, digestive system, cardiovascular system, renal system, endocrine system, nervous system, musculoskeletal system, exocrine system, glymphatic system, lymphatic system, immune system, and sexual system) soul, spirit heart, decisions, worship, destiny, offices, business, and relationships, in the Name of Jesus.

I praise You now for freedom, newness of life, and empowerment from You, Holy Spirit. I thank You for setting me free and I pray that barricades would now be set up preventing all attempts at retaliatory efforts. In doing so I activate Your Word on behalf of my life and the lives of my loved ones.

I declare, Lord God, that You are my Shield, Buckler, Rear Guard, Strong Tower, and Fortress. I put my trust and faith in You, Lord Jesus.

I seal this prayer to a realm of timelessness and anchor it to every realm, age, timeline, dimension, planet, cosmos, and universe, past, present, and future, to infinity, and from the beginning across eternity.

Any attacks because of this Word, these prayers, declarations or deliverance, backfire, in the Name of Jesus. *Amen.*

Dear Reader

Thank you for acquiring and reading this book. If you've had the displeasure of experiencing an unfriendly friend or more than one – a gang up in the natural or in the spiritual realm, I pray the Lord will stop them for your sake.

Review the Courts of Heaven prayers and pray them until you get release and deliverance, in the Name of Jesus.

Amen.

Dr. Marlene Miles

Other books by this author

(related or mentioned titles are pictured with links)

AK: The Adventures of the *Agape* Kid

AMONG SOME THIEVES

Ancestral Powers

Backstabbers

Blindsided: *Has the Old Man Bewitched You?*

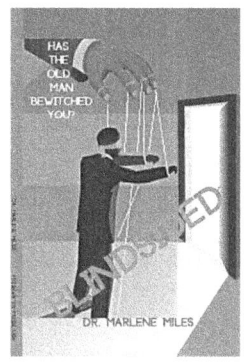

https://a.co/d/5O2fLLR

Churchzilla, The Wanna-Be, Supposed-to-be Bride of Christ

Darkness

Demons Hate Questions

Devil Weapons: Unforgiveness, Bitterness,...

Dream Defilement
https://a.co/d/4f4P3Et

Don't Refuse Me, Lord (4 book series)

Every Evil Bird

Evil Touch

Failed Assignment

Fantasy Spirit Spouse

FAT Demons (The): *Breaking Demonic Curses*

The Fold (4 book series)

- The Fold (Book 1)
- Name Your Seed (Book 2)
- The Poor Attitudes of Money (3)
- Do Not Orphan Your Seed

got HEALING? Verses for Life

got LOVE? Verses for Life

got HOPE? Verses for Life

got money?

How to Dental Assist

How to Dental Assit2: Be Productive, Not Wasteful

Let Me Have A Dollar's Worth

Living for the NOW of God
https://a.co/d/1pwGkJJ

Lose My Location
https://a.co/d/crD6mV9

Man Safari, *The (mini book)*

Marriage Ed. Rules of Engagement & Marriage

Made Perfect in Love

Motherboard (The) - soul prosperity series

Plantation Souls

Power Money: Nine Times the Tithe

The Power of Wealth *(forthcoming)*

Seasons of Grief

Seasons of War

Sift You Like Wheat

Soul Prosperity soul prosperity series 3

https://a.co/d/5p8YvCN

Souls Captivity soul prosperity series 2

The Spirit of Poverty

This Is NOT That: How to Keep Demons from Coming At You

Throne of Grace: Courtroom Prayer

Time Is of the Essence
https://a.co/d/1w4V5o9

Too Many Wives: *Why You Have Lady Problems*

Tormenting Spirits
https://a.co/d/dAogEJf

Triangular Power *(series)*

- Powers Above
- SUNBLOCK
- Do Not Swear by the Moon
- STARSTRUCK

Uncontested Doom

Upgrade: How to Get Out of Survival Mode

- **Toxic Souls** (Book 2 of series)
- **Legacy** (Book 3 of series)

Warfare Prayer Against Beauty Curses

Warfare Prayer Against Poverty

What Have You to Declare?

When the Devourer is Rebuked (mini book)

When You See Blood
https://a.co/d/apvdjvW

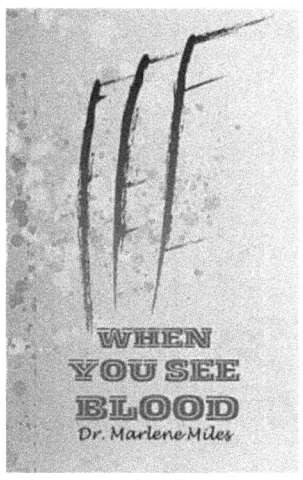

The Wilderness Romance *(series)*

- *The Social Wilderness*
- *The Sexual Wilderness*
- *The Spiritual Wilderness*

Without Form
https://a.co/d/4pV9abm

Series

The Fold (a series on Godly finances)
https://a.co/d/4hz3unj

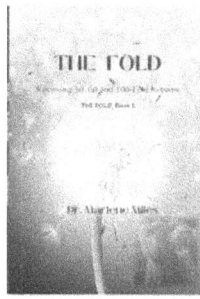  

Soul Prosperity Series https://a.co/d/bz2M42q

Spirit Spouse books

https://a.co/d/9VehDSo

https://a.co/d/97sKOwm

 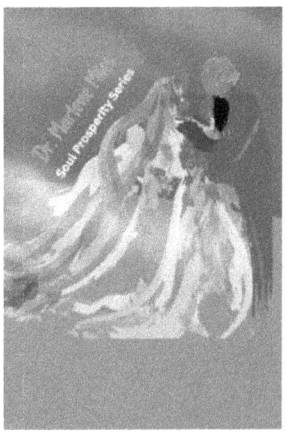

Thieves of Darkness series

Triangular Powers https://a.co/d/aUCjAWC

Upgrade (series) *How to Get Out of Survival Mode* https://a.co/d/aTERhXO

www.ingramcontent.com/pod-product-compliance
Lightning Source LLC
Chambersburg PA
CBHW070853050426
42453CB00012B/2178